WORKING TOWARD GAINING

EQUALITY
FOR
WOMEN

Cynthia O'Brien

CRABTREE
PUBLISHING COMPANY
WWW.CRABTREEBOOKS.COM

CRABTREE
PUBLISHING COMPANY
WWW.CRABTREEBOOKS.COM

Author: Cynthia O'Brien
Picture Manager: Sophie Mortimer
Designer: Lynne Lennon
Design Manager: Keith Davis
Children's Publisher: Anne O'Daly
Editorial director: Kathy Middleton
Editor: Janine Deschenes
Proofreader: Wendy Scavuzzo
Print coordinator: Katherine Berti

Copyright © Brown Bear
Books Ltd 2020

Photographs: (t=top, b= bottom, l=left, r=right, c=center)

Front Cover: Alamy: Pacific Press Agency (center right); Shutterstock: JessicaGirvan1 (bottom center) Sundry Photography (bottom left); Wikimedia Commons: Adèle Goodman Clark Papers, Special Collections and Archives, VCU Libraries (center left)

Interior: Alamy: Entertainment Pictures 33, Joerg Boething 35, The Granger Historical Picture Archive 7t, 20, 21t, North Wind Picture Archives 10, Pictorial Press Ltd 9b, 18, Trinity Mirror/Mirrorpix 22; Associated Press: Christoph Soeder/picture-alliance/dpa 11; British Library: 14; Getty Images: Bettmann 17t, The New York Historical Society 25; Lynn Gilbert 24; Kvennafri.is: 29; Library of Congress: 8, 13, 26; Mark Lloyd: 17b; National Portrait Gallery: 12; Public Domain: gaelx 32, FW Mason 9t, MNH 15, Alfred Pearce 19, Southbank Centre 30, Women's March on Washington 37; Shutterstock: Sebastian Barros 5, rob Crandall 34, Everett Collection 16, Sheila Fitzgerald 1, Ali Hasan 39t, leoks 6, David Mbiyu 38, Nabil Mohsen 23, Joyce Nelson 21b, jess Pomponio 41t, Lev Radin 36, 39b, 41b, Johnny Silvercloud 43, Stock Photo World 4; U.S. Government: 27, JFK Presidential Library and Museum/Abbie Rowe 28, White House/Pete Souza 31, WHTV/Clinton Presidential Library 7b.

Brown Bear Books has made every attempt to contact the copyright holder. If you have any information about omissions, please contact licensing@brownbearbooks.co.uk

Library and Archives Canada Cataloging in Publication

Title: Working toward gaining equality for women / Cynthia O'Brien.
Names: O'Brien, Cynthia (Cynthia J.), author.
Description: Series statement: Achieving social change | Includes bibliographical references and index.
Identifiers: Canadiana (print) 20200300318 | Canadiana (ebook) 20200300326 | ISBN 9780778779452 (hardcover) | ISBN 9780778779513 (softcover) | ISBN 9781427125491 (HTML)
Subjects: LCSH: Women's rights—Juvenile literature. | LCSH: Equality—Juvenile literature. | LCSH: Sex discrimination against women—Juvenile literature.
Classification: LCC HQ1236 .O27 2021 | DDC j305.42—dc23

Library of Congress Cataloging-in-Publication Data

Names: O'Brien, Cynthia (Cynthia J.) author.
Title: Working toward gaining equality for women / Cynthia O'Brien.
Description: New York : Crabtree Publishing Company, 2021. | Series: Achieving social change | Includes bibliographical references and index.
Identifiers: LCCN 2020032436 (print) | LCCN 2020032437 (ebook) | ISBN 9780778779452 (hardcover) | ISBN 9780778779513 (paperback) | ISBN 9781427125491 (ebook)
Subjects: LCSH: Women's rights--Juvenile literature. | Equality--Juvenile literature. | Sex discrimination against women.--Juvenile literature.
Classification: LCC HQ1236 .O27 2021 (print) | LCC HQ1236 (ebook) | DDC 305.42--dc23
LC record available at https://lccn.loc.gov/2020032436
LC ebook record available at https://lccn.loc.gov/2020032437

Crabtree Publishing Company
www.crabtreebooks.com   1-800-387-7650

Published in Canada
Crabtree Publishing
616 Welland Ave.
St. Catharines, ON
L2M 5V6

Published in the United States
Crabtree Publishing
347 Fifth Ave
Suite 1402-145
New York, NY 10016

Published by CRABTREE PUBLISHING COMPANY in 2021

Printed in the U.S.A./092020/CG20200810

CONTENTS

INTRODUCTION

Women have faced discrimination in almost every area of life. For many years, they were not allowed to get an education, own property, or vote. Women are often paid less money than men for the same work. They also face violence because of their gender. Women's rights activists are people who fight these injustices.

Activists are the people who try to bring about social change. This change can be within a community or across a country. Activists **campaign** to force organizations or governments to change practices or laws. They also campaign to change attitudes and raise awareness about injustices. Their campaigns involve many **tactics**, from posters and social media to large marches, protests, and demonstrations.

Activists include high-profile figures such as Michelle Obama, who use their voices to draw attention to women's rights.

A Long Struggle

Achieving social change does not happen quickly. Over hundreds of years, people have worked to address many issues. Some issues are ongoing, while new ones arise. This means that activists carry on the work of those before them while fighting against new injustices.

Rights for Women

For many years, women's rights activists have fought for issues including education, voting, and equal pay. Although women now have these rights in many countries, there are more challenges to overcome. Women still earn less than men and are more likely to be victims of violence. Women of color, trans women, and women with a disability face additional discrimination. Activists keep working toward a better future.

Women in Colombia perform a song and dance that protests male violence against women. First performed in Chile, the song spread across the world through social media.

CHAPTER 1

WHAT ARE WOMEN'S RIGHTS?

Women's rights have changed throughout history. In ancient Greece, for example, most women had no political power. In North America, before contact with settlers, many Indigenous cultures had a balanced view of women's and men's rights.

The women's rights movement has been created by millions of activists and has taken many forms. Early feminists did not go on public marches, but they found other ways to raise awareness about women's rights. French writer Marie de Gournay wrote *Equality of Men and Women*. This was a radical idea in 1622. De Gournay also translated texts into Latin to demonstrate that women could and should be educated, just like men.

Rights in ancient Egypt depended on social class, not gender. Higher class women could own and manage property and represent themselves in court.

American activist Amelia Bloomer was part of the first wave of **feminism**. She created a newspaper called The Lily that published articles about women's rights.

Four Waves

Since the 1800s, there have been four major waves of feminism. The first wave, from the mid-1800s to early 1900s, was mainly about women's rights to property and voting. The second wave, in the 1960s and 1970s, focused on new goals such as the right to equal pay. The 1990s brought the third wave that was more **inclusive** and took account of women's overlapping identities, such as race and gender. Around 2012, a fourth wave began. It uses new tactics, such as social media campaigns, to advance women's rights in the 21st century.

Key Voices

Wilma Mankiller

In 1985, Wilma Mankiller became the first female Principal Chief of the Cherokee Nation. She reminded people that women had held positions of authority in Indigenous nations before the arrival of European settlers. As Chief, she built health clinics and introduced education and job training programs.

Issues of Race and Culture

Women have faced discrimination due to their gender throughout history. But many women also faced discrimination due to their race, culture, class, or religion. They still do today.

Black women fought against **racism** for many years. In the 1800s, they also fought for women's right to vote. Mary Church Terrell became one of the first African-American women to graduate from college. However, she and other Black **suffragists** were not always welcome in White organizations. In 1896, Terrell and others formed the National Association of Colored Women (NACW). The organization's motto was "Lifting as we climb." It fought for women's rights but also campaigned against **lynchings** and worked for improvements to education.

Mary Church Terrell was the only Black woman to speak at the International Congress of Women in Germany in 1904. She gave her speech in English, German, and French.

Indigenous Women

Indigenous activists in North America have fought, and continue to fight, for their rights to land sovereignty and equal opportunities. Women such as Sara Winnemucca, a Paiute, gave talks and wrote about the impact white settlement had on Indigenous life, including women's rights. In New Zealand, European settlement affected Māori culture and women's rights. After European settlement, Māori women were no longer considered equal leaders in their communities. Activists such as Meri Te Tai Mangakāhia fought for Māori women's rights.

> *Meri Te Tai Mangakāhia wanted women to have the right to vote and to stand as candidates in the Māori Parliament.*

Key Voices

Sojourner Truth

In 1851, Sojourner Truth gave a rousing speech at the Women's Rights Convention in Akron, Ohio. Truth, a former enslaved person, spoke passionately in support of women's right to vote and against **slavery**. She inspired others to join the fight for **suffrage**.

9

Financial Rights

Women have often been denied rights to money and property. In England, the law of coverture gave a married man complete control over his wife and her property.

This carried over to the North American colonies. Change was slow, and states introduced changes at different times. From 1839, the Married Women's Property Acts started to give women more control over their property. Activists such as Isabella Beecher Hooker pushed for change. By 1900, married women in all states could own property, just like men could. However, property rights were mainly granted to White women.

Women in colonial America (1607 to 1776) had few rights. When they married, control over any property they owned passed to their husbands.

Money and Banking

The fight to gain control over money took longer. In the United States in the 1960s, banks could refuse to give single women a credit card, and married women needed their husband's consent. This continued until 1974. France gave single women the right to open a bank account in 1881 and married women in 1886. Women in the United States and Canada had to wait until the 1960s.

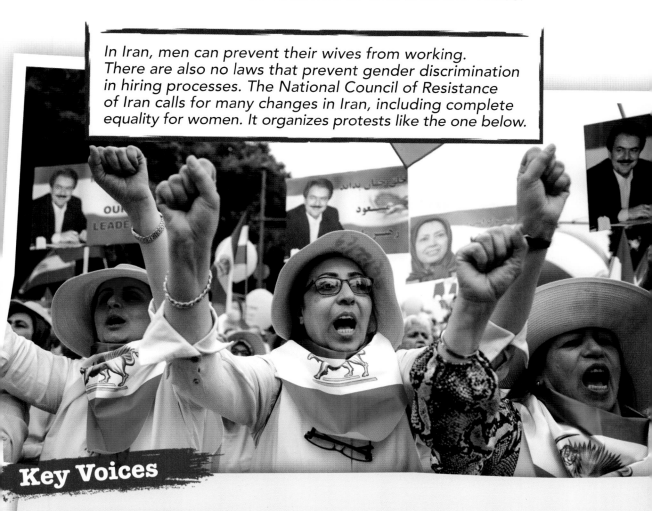

In Iran, men can prevent their wives from working. There are also no laws that prevent gender discrimination in hiring processes. The National Council of Resistance of Iran calls for many changes in Iran, including complete equality for women. It organizes protests like the one below.

Key Voices

Marilyn Waring

The New Zealand activist and **economist**, Marilyn Waring became the country's youngest member of parliament in 1975. She wrote *If Women Counted* in 1988. She pointed out that politicians don't give economic value to women's housework and caring for family members. Waring is known as the founder of feminist economics.

CHAPTER 2

EARLY FEMINISTS

English writer, Mary Wollstonecraft, published her famous book, *A Vindication of the Rights of Woman*, in 1792. She argued that women were just as capable as men and should have the same rights to education.

While her brother received a formal education and attended school, Wollstonecraft did not. This was not unusual for women at the time. Instead, Wollstonecraft learned by reading as much as she could. Her family had no money, so she had to find work. Wollstonecraft worked as a **lady's companion** at first, but she was passionate about education. In 1784, she helped to establish a school in London with her sister and her best friend. Three years later, Wollstonecraft wrote *Thoughts on the Education of Daughters*. The school did not earn money and eventually closed down. In 1788, Wollstonecraft began earning some money with her writing. Four years later, she wrote her most famous work.

Wollstonecraft's views were controversial. One male politician at the time called her "a hyena in **petticoats**."

> I do not wish them [women] to have power over men; but over themselves.
>
> Mary Wollstonecraft

Planned as the first volume of three, but the only one to be written, *Vindication was a passionate argument for the education of women.*

VINDICATION

OF THE

RIGHTS OF WOMAN:

WITH

STRICTURES

ON

POLITICAL AND MORAL SUBJECTS.

BY MARY WOLLSTONECRAFT.

PRINTED AT *BOSTON*,
BY PETER EDES FOR THOMAS AND ANDREWS,
FAUST's Statue, No. 45, Newbury-Street.
MDCCXCII.

A Hard Life

Wollstonecraft's life was full of struggle. It was not easy to make money as a woman, but she carved out a career as a writer. She did not marry the father of her first child. At the time, most people disapproved of that. People also disapproved of her ideas in *A Vindication of the Rights of Woman.* But the work sold many copies and caused people to talk about women's rights. Wollstonecraft died in 1797, when her second child was only ten days old. Although her book didn't lead to change in her lifetime, her work and life inspired later women's rights activists, including Elizabeth Cady Stanton and Lucretia Mott.

Power of the Pen

Opportunities for early feminists were limited. The main routes for women were marriage or the church. Despite this, some women were able to raise awareness about women's rights through their writing.

Christine de Pisan was born in 1364. Unlike many women at the time, de Pisan had been well educated. After her husband and father died, de Pisan supported herself and her family through her writing. As she grew older, she turned her attention to women's rights, particularly the right to education. Her book *The Book of the City of Ladies*, published in 1405, celebrated the achievements of women. De Pisan's work influenced other women writers such as the Italian writer Laura Cereta. Cereta also believed that women should be given the same education as men.

This painting shows de Pisan lecturing a group of men, a highly unusual act for the time.

The Right to Learn

In Mexico, Sor Juana Inés de la Cruz became a nun. That allowed her to focus on her education and to write. She was passionate about women's right to learn. By the 1690s, Sor Juana was famous in Mexico and Spain, but her writings angered the Catholic Church. She defended her ideas, but the Church forced Sor Juana to get rid of all her books and to stop writing. Centuries after her death in 1695, Sor Juana has inspired many books and a film about her life.

Sor Juana's poetry addressed subjects such as women's rights and relationships between women and men.

Key Voices

Olympe de Gouges

In 1789, French revolutionaries replaced their king with a government of citizens. The revolution's motto was "Liberty, Equality, Brotherhood." Olympe de Gouges was a French advocate of women's rights. In 1791, she published the *Declaration of the Rights of Women and of the Female Citizen*. She argued that the Revolution excluded women from equal rights. In 1793, de Gouges was executed for opposing the government.

Taking up the Cause

In the late 1700s and early 1800s, women's rights activists did not gather in large, organized groups. Women wrote and gave or attended lectures. **They worked in small groups. Sometimes, they used their husband's positions to get their messages across.**

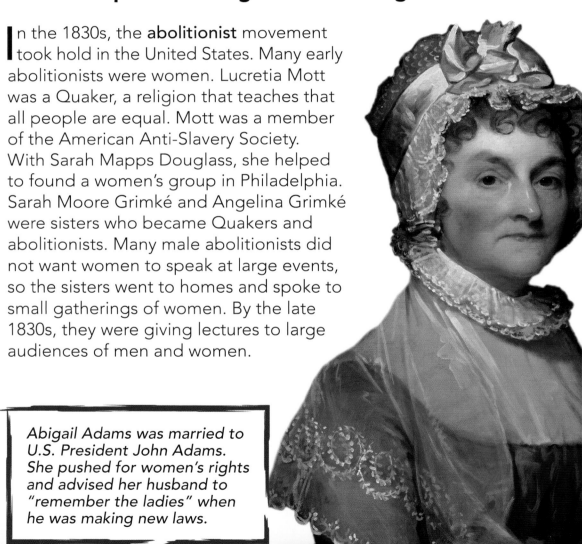

In the 1830s, the **abolitionist** movement took hold in the United States. Many early abolitionists were women. Lucretia Mott was a Quaker, a religion that teaches that all people are equal. Mott was a member of the American Anti-Slavery Society. With Sarah Mapps Douglass, she helped to found a women's group in Philadelphia. Sarah Moore Grimké and Angelina Grimké were sisters who became Quakers and abolitionists. Many male abolitionists did not want women to speak at large events, so the sisters went to homes and spoke to small gatherings of women. By the late 1830s, they were giving lectures to large audiences of men and women.

Abigail Adams was married to U.S. President John Adams. She pushed for women's rights and advised her husband to "remember the ladies" when he was making new laws.

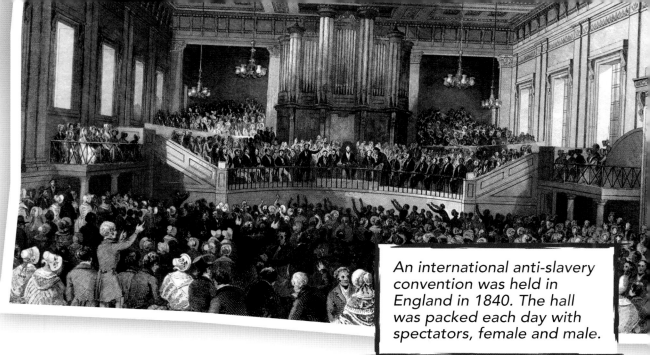

An international anti-slavery convention was held in England in 1840. The hall was packed each day with spectators, female and male.

Equality for All

The abolitionist movement aimed to end slavery, but it also sought equality between Black and White people. Women like Lucretia Mott and Elizabeth Cady Stanton began thinking that they should organize a movement that focused on equality for women. Women in Britain were thinking the same thing. This was the start of the first wave of feminism.

Key Voices

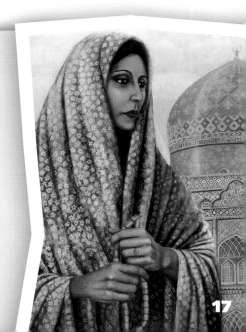

Táhirih

Activist and poet Fatimah Baraghani, known as Táhirih, was born in 1814 in Persia, now Iran. Women at that time were not allowed to show their faces in public. In 1848, Táhirih spoke at a meeting of men about rejecting old traditions. She caused outrage when she removed her veil to speak. In 1852, Táhirih was executed for her beliefs and activities.

CHAPTER 3

GETTING THE VOTE

Women campaigned for the right to vote throughout the 1800s. These suffragists used peaceful tactics. By the early 1900s, however, some activists had run out of patience.

They decided **militant** action was the way to get their voices heard. In 1903, Emmeline Pankhurst founded the Women's Social and Political Union (WSPU) in Britain. Their motto was "Deeds Not Words." They organized militant actions, including breaking windows and handcuffing themselves to railings. Many **suffragettes** were arrested and put in prison. Some of the women protested by going on hunger strike (refusing to eat) in prison. The guards force-fed the hunger strikers. This was a violent action that involved holding the women down and forcing a rubber tube into the nose or throat.

Emmeline Pankhurst was arrested many times for her protests. She went on a hunger strike to improve the conditions for imprisoned suffragettes.

> "We were willing to break laws that we might force men to give us the right to make laws."
> Emmeline Pankhurst

This poster, produced by the WSPU, showed the violent methods used to force-feed suffragette prisoners. It raised awareness about what suffragettes faced.

"Cat and Mouse"

The government didn't want the women to die in prison. In 1913, it introduced an act to try to deal with the hunger strikers. The new law allowed the women to be released temporarily, get healthy again, and then be re-arrested. It became known as the "Cat and Mouse Act." The new law didn't stop the suffragettes. They continued their campaign, and the cruel treatment of the women sparked public anger and support for their cause. In 1914, World War I broke out in Europe, and the suffragettes set aside their protests to join the war effort. They took on many of the jobs that were normally done by men. When the war ended in 1918, some women in the United Kingdom—such as those over 30 years old or who were university graduates—were given the vote.

Coming Together

In July 1848, Lucretia Mott and Elizabeth Cady Stanton organized a Women's Rights Convention in Seneca Falls, New York. Speakers demanded women's rights to get an education, own property, and to vote.

The Seneca Falls convention launched the campaign for American suffrage. One of the campaign's leaders was Susan B. Anthony. Although she didn't attend the convention, she met Elizabeth Cady Stanton and they became good friends. They traveled around the country, speaking up for women's rights and the right to vote. In 1872, Anthony was arrested for voting illegally. She was taken to court and fined $100. The sentence made many people angry and boosted Anthony's cause.

Elizabeth Cady Stanton speaking at the Women's Rights Convention. Among the Convention's demands was a woman's right to vote.

A Call to Action

In England, Harriet Taylor Mill was inspired by the American suffragists. In 1851, she wrote an essay as a call to action, "The Enfranchisement of Women." In 1866, her husband, John Stuart Mill, presented a **petition** calling for women's voting rights. More than 1,500 people signed it, but nothing happened. Three years later, he published an essay, "The Subjection of Women," that argued for women's rights in general. Mill worked on the original ideas for the essay with Harriet. He carried on working on it after her death in 1858.

Harriet Taylor Mill was a thinker and writer in her own right. She also made major contributions to her husband 's work.

Key Voices

Nellie McClung

Nellie McClung was part of the "Famous Five," a group of women activists who applied to Canada's Supreme Court in 1927. The group wanted the court to declare women as "persons," who could serve in government. The following year, women in Canada were officially "persons." In 1930, Cairine Reay Wilson was the first woman appointed to the Senate.

Votes for All Women

Most women in the United States won the right to vote in 1920. However, the new laws did not include Black women. The Voting Rights Act, which banned racial discrimination, was not passed until 1965. In Canada, most women could vote in 1918. But Indigenous women, the last to receive this right, could not vote until 1960.

Around the world, women won the vote at different times and in different ways. By the early 1900s, the right to vote was a global issue. In the UK, the 1918 Representation of the People Act gave the right to vote to women over 30 who owned property of a certain value. It wasn't until 1928 that the voting age for women was lowered to 21, giving them equality with men.

"Women's Sunday" was a suffragette march and rally held in London in 1908. Up to half a million women and men attended.

VOTES for WOMEN

A young woman votes in an election in Egypt in 2018. Decades of activism by earlier Egyptian women had won the vote for women.

Votes for Some, But Not for All

While American women were granted the right to vote in 1920, Native American people could not vote until 1924—four years later. Indigenous voting rights in Australia and Canada were ignored for decades. In Canada, Indigenous peoples were excluded from the vote until 1960. Australia gave White women the right to vote in 1902, but Aboriginal and Torres Strait Islander people in the country could not vote until the mid-1960s.

Activism forced change in other countries. Huda Sha'arawi founded the Egyptian Feminist Union in 1923. Almost 30 years later, Doria Shafik and a group of 1,500 women gathered at the government buildings to demand voting rights. Egyptian women won the right to vote in 1956.

Key Events

Suffrage in New Zealand

In 1893, New Zealand became the first nation to allow women to vote. The suffrage movement there began in the late 1860s and included many petitions to government. Finally, almost 32,000 people signed the petition in 1893. The government passed the bill in September, giving all adult women the right to vote, including Indigenous women.

CHAPTER 4

FIGHTING FOR RIGHTS

On August 26, 1970, more than 50,000 women and some men marched down Fifth Avenue in New York City. Another 100,000 women protested in cities across the United States. The march marked 50 years since American women won the right to vote.

Betty Friedan organized the event. In 1963, she wrote *The Feminine Mystique*. Her book challenged the idea of traditional women's roles, including the fact that women were expected to do more domestic chores than men. Three years later, Friedan helped to found the National Organization for Women (NOW). NOW sponsored the August 26 event. Friedan's idea was to ask all women to go on **strike** for the day. This included stopping housework, such as ironing and cooking, to show how much was done by women.

Betty Friedan's book became a bestseller and is often credited as starting the second wave of feminism.

Who knows what women can be when they are finally able to become themselves?
Betty Friedan

Women's Strike for Equality

On the day of the **strike**, women from all different backgrounds came together. Young and older women marched, holding banners calling for equality and for women to unite. The organizers also arranged sit-ins, a type of protest in which a group of people take over a space. Women went into men-only clubs, organized speeches, and held **rallies**. The activists were fighting for demands including more childcare centers, and equal opportunities in education and work. Over the next few years, protestors used various tactics— from protests to influencing politicians— to try to achieve these aims.

Many of the protestors had also taken part in **civil rights** marches and anti-war protests. The women's strike brought these activists together. The protests also called attention to these issues as a result.

WOMEN STRIKE FOR PEACE- AND EQUALITY!

FOR PEACE AND EQUALITY!

I'M NO BREEDER FOR THE MAN'S WAR!

SISTERHOOD IS POWERFUL- END THE WAR! WOMEN STRIKE FOR PEACE.

THE WOMEN OF VIETNAM ARE OUR SISTERS WOMEN STRIKE FOR PEACE

A New Wave Begins

At the Women's Strike for Equality in 1970, Kate Millett declared, "We're a movement now." This second wave of feminism began in the United States, then spread to other parts of the world.

By the 1960s, many women were better educated than in the past. But universities such as Yale and Princeton did not accept women until 1969. Through protests and petitions, activists pushed for changes. In the United States, government acts made it illegal for schools to discriminate on the basis of gender. The Sex Discrimination Act of 1975 in Britain also included education. The Canadian Human Rights Act of 1977 made it illegal to discriminate against women because of their sex.

The Women's Liberation Movement in the 1960s and 1970s was part of the second wave of feminism. Groups such as the National Organization for Women (NOW) pushed for equality in all areas of women's lives.

Women's Rights and Civil Rights

Race continued to be an issue in the fight for women's rights. Non-white women faced additional discrimination. As a result, many women's rights activists also joined the civil rights movement in the United States. Dorothy Height helped to organize the March on Washington, in 1963, a major protest for civil rights. She was also president of the National Council of Negro Women, which advocated for Black women's rights. Height worked for women's education rights and encouraged women to use their vote.

Dorothy Height, pictured (right) with Eleanor Roosevelt, said the three best ways to fight for justice were to "**agitate**, agitate, agitate."

Key Voices

Mary Two-Axe Earley

Mary Two-Axe Earley was a member of the Mohawk nation in Canada. From the 1960s through the 1970s, she was a pioneer of the women's rights movement and battled to gain rights for Indigenous women. She fought against laws that said a woman would lose her **status** as a **First Nations** person if she married a man without status or was divorced from a man with status. Without status, a woman could not own **reserve** property or pass on status to her children. In 1985, the Canadian government changed the law, giving legal rights to Indigenous women.

Equal Pay

Traditionally, women were paid less than men, even when they were doing the same jobs. Women are more likely to work part time to raise children or take jobs with lower pay.

In the 1960s, women pushed for changes. They included Esther Peterson, director of the Women's Bureau in the Department of Labor, who drafted the Equal Pay Act. In 1968 in the UK, 850 women sewing machinists at the Ford car factory in Dagenham went on strike. They had found out that they were being paid less than men doing equivalent work. The women's demands paved the way for the Equal Pay Act of 1970. This said that men and women should be paid the same for doing the same work.

President Kennedy signs the Equal Pay Act into law in 1963. This was one of the first laws that addressed gender discrimination.

Icelandic Women's Strike

On October 24, 1975, a group of 25,000 women gathered in Reykjavik, the capital city of Iceland. They were protesting against pay inequality for women. The women did not go to work or do any housework or childcare that day. The strike started to change attitudes about women's work. Five years later, Iceland elected its first woman president, Vigdés Finnbogadéttir.

The Icelandic Women's Strike involved 90 percent of the country's women.

A Constitutional Change

Another proposal in the United States was the Equal Rights **Amendment** (ERA) of 1972. This had its roots in the suffrage movement. The amendment was first introduced in 1923 and asserted that women and men would have equal rights under the law. However, the campaign didn't gain enough support. In the 1960s, the ERA became a focus for second-wave feminists. Congress passed the ERA in 1972, but the amendment needed to be **ratified** by three quarters of all states within seven years to become law. Many states did not ratify the proposal. Today, activist groups such as the ERA Coalition are pushing for the ERA to become law.

CHAPTER 5

THE FIGHT GOES ON

In 2012, 15-year-old schoolgirl Malala Yousafzai was traveling home from school by bus in Pakistan. A masked gunman boarded the bus and shouted, "Who is Malala?" When he identified the girl, the gunman fired. He hit Malala on the left side of her head.

Doctors treated Malala in Pakistan, then flew her to England for surgery. Four years earlier, Malala was an 11-year-old schoolgirl. The **Taliban** had taken control of her town in Pakistan in 2007. The group banned many things, including education for girls. Malala spoke out. In September 2008, she gave a speech, "How Dare the Taliban Take Away My Basic Right to Education?" A few months later, she started writing a diary for a British online news website. She used the name Gul Makai to disguise her identity. But her identity became known. In 2009, Pakistan's army forced the Taliban out, but the Taliban remained hiding in the hills near Malala's home.

After recovering from her injuries, Malala continued her education in the UK. She graduated from Oxford University in 2020.

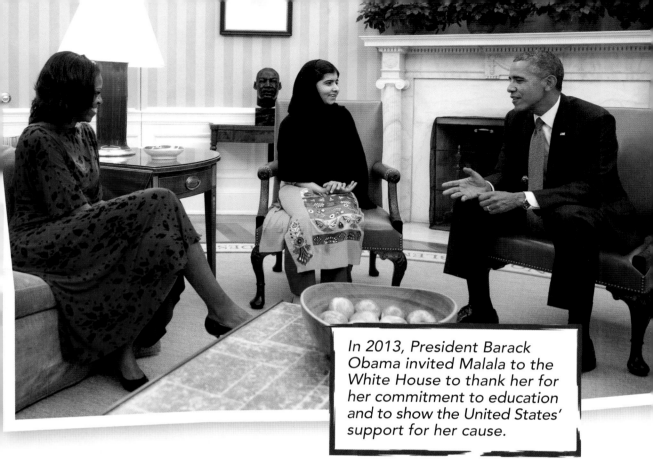

In 2013, President Barack Obama invited Malala to the White House to thank her for her commitment to education and to show the United States' support for her cause.

Nobel Prize

In 2013, Malala gave a speech at the United Nations Headquarters in New York. She asked world leaders to act for girls' education and women's rights. The same year, Malala and her father started the Malala Fund, which raises money to help girls go to school. The next year, Malala received the Nobel Peace Prize that recognized her bravery and activism. She was the youngest winner ever. Malala continues her activism. Her fund builds schools in refugee camps and in countries, such as Iraq, that have been devastated by war.

> If one man can destroy everything, why can't one girl change it?
> Malala Yousafzai

A New Feminism

The third wave of feminism arrived around 1990. Activists from the 1960s until the 1990s had helped bring about big changes. Women who were born during these times were enjoying some of the benefits of these changes, including better education and jobs.

Some women criticized feminism for not being inclusive enough. These third-wave feminists wanted their version of feminism to embrace individuality and diversity. These activists drew attention to the different experiences and challenges faced by women of different races, economic classes, sexualities, and more. In 1989, lawyer and civil rights activist Kimberlé Crenshaw used the term "intersectionality" to draw attention to the ways that different oppressions overlap. In particular, Black feminists pointed out that they experienced discrimination because of their race as well as their gender. Intersectionality was an important part of third-wave feminism.

Writer and academic Rebecca Walker was one of the founders of the third wave of feminism. She is a co-founder of the Third Wave Fund, which supports young women activists in political campaigns.

Key Voices

Guerrilla Girls

The Guerrilla Girls is a group of activists and artists. Members wear gorilla masks to remain **anonymous**. The group formed in 1985 to work for equality in the art world. In the 1990s, it expanded its protests to government. Activists made posters that target large art galleries, such as the Metropolitan Museum in New York City, for displaying mainly men's art.

A Global Fight

Meanwhile, women's rights became even more of a global fight. In 1995, people from many countries gathered in China for the World Conference on Women. The conference ended with a declaration for action on equality, stating that human rights are women's rights. Five years later, the United Nations called for women to be involved in peacekeeping missions. Later, in 2010, UN Women formed as a group to empower women and work for equality and rights.

While many second-wave feminists fought against traditional roles by rejecting feminine clothing, some third-wave feminists used a feminine appearance to show the power to choose their own self-expression. This was labeled the "new girl power." The group Spice Girls, formed in 1994, helped popularize this girl power in the media.

Women Stand Up

In 1991, American lawyer Anita Hill accused judge Clarence Thomas of sexual harassment. Hill spoke out against Thomas's appointment to the U.S. Supreme Court. Many people accused Hill of lying, however, and Thomas was appointed.

Anita Hill was questioned by an all-male, all-White committee. She spoke out at a time when few accusations of sexual harassment went to court. Hill's case made headlines around the world. It sparked widespread awareness and anger about sexual harassment in the workplace. Just one month after Hill spoke out, the U.S. Congress passed a law to extend the rights of victims of sexual harassment in the workplace. It gave them the right to a jury trial, for example. And following the trial, more women came forward to report their own complaints of sexual harassment.

Hill's courage in speaking out inspired others and showed women that they didn't have to put up with sexual harassment.

Key Events

Marches for Women's Lives

In 1992, around 750,000 activists marched in Washington, DC. They pushed the Supreme Court to uphold the right to choose to have an abortion. Later, in 2004, more than 1 million people marched for women's **reproductive rights**. Both marches were organized by the National Organization for Women (NOW).

Taking Action

Anita Hill showed that women can stand up to those in power. Her example was carried forward in other parts of the world. Many women took direct action against sexual harassment by those in power. In 2006, the Gulabi Gang formed in Uttar Pradesh, a state in northern India. The founder of the group, Sampat Pal Devi, saw a man beating his wife. When Devi tried to stop him, she was beaten as well. The next day, she came back with five other women. She brought a lathi (stick) and attacked the man. From a small, local group, the movement grew to include more than 400,000 members. The women, dressed in pink, protest against domestic violence and forced marriages and organize activities that bring women together.

Gulabi Gang members, carrying sticks, tackle violence against women, especially those in poor areas.

CHAPTER 6

FEMINIST ACTIVISM TODAY

There is no agreement about when, or even if, a fourth wave of feminism began. But a shift started around 2012, when Laura Bates started the Everyday Sexism Project.

Feminists, still focusing on inclusivity and intersectionality, began to use new tools to fight injustice. Bates used the Internet to spread her message. She asked women and girls to share examples of the type of sexism they experienced each day. Though some people use social media for the wrong reasons, it has become a forceful tool for women's rights issues. Through social media, activists have the power to raise awareness immediately. At the same time, there are more women's rights organizations today than ever before. They use social media to gather support. They also work in local communities, helping women to start businesses, organizing petitions, and providing legal or financial support.

Nigerian writer Chimamanda Ngozi Adichie presented a TED talk that then turned into a book. We Should All Be Feminists *argued that feminism benefits all people and should be a priority in the 21st Century.*

Looking Back, Looking Forward

The powerful words and actions of past activists inspire today's campaigners. In many parts of the world, women have gained legal equality, but not social equality. Fourth-wave feminists are working toward wide, inclusive aims that recognize that women's rights are human rights.

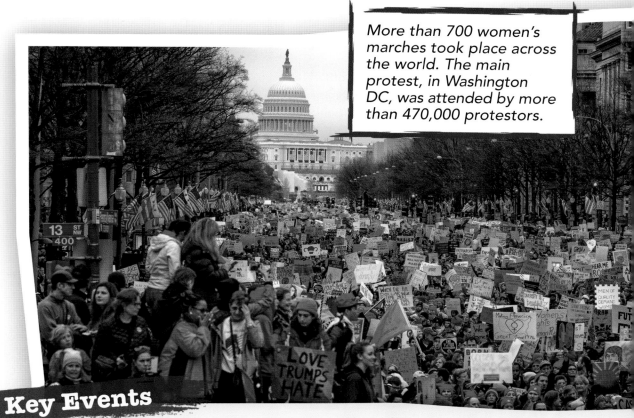

More than 700 women's marches took place across the world. The main protest, in Washington DC, was attended by more than 470,000 protestors.

Key Events

Global Women's Marches

On January 21, 2017, between 3.5 and 4.6 million people took part in the Women's March in the United States. The event started as a single Facebook post by retired lawyer Teresa Shook. It was a reaction to the election of President Donald Trump. Activists were alarmed by sexist comments he had made during his presidential campaign, and feared that his policies would roll back women's rights. Around 5 million more activists, mostly women, took part in marches around the world. The protestors marched for women's rights, but also for equality for everyone.

Ending Violence

Violence against women is not a new problem. Today's activists work in groups in their local communities and in government. They also take part in worldwide campaigns.

The 16 Days of Activism Against Gender-Based Violence is an annual, global event. It draws attention to the fact that women are more likely to be the victims of violence than men. The Bring Back Our Girls campaign also gathered global support. It was set up in 2014, in response to **Boko Haram's** kidnapping of 276 girls from their school in Chibok, Nigeria. It started as a one-day march in Nigeria, but was turned into a global media campaign by Nigerian Minister for Education Obiageli Ezekwesili.

The #BringBackOurGirls protest spread around the world. In 2020, 112 of the girls were still missing.

Hashtag Protest

The "Me Too" movement was started by Tarana Burke in 2006. Burke worked to support survivors of sexual violence and wanted to show them they were not alone. The movement got global attention in October 2017 when the actor Alyssa Milano sent out a tweet asking that anyone who had been sexually harassed or **assaulted** should use the hashtag #MeToo. In just days, more than 12 million people had done so. Powerful figures such as movie producer Harvey Weinstein and comedian Bill Cosby were accused and convicted of their crimes—major victories for the Me Too movement.

Women journalists launched the #MeToo movement in Bangladesh in October 2018. Just as in the rest of the world, Bangladeshi women took to social media to accuse men, many in powerful positions, of sexual harassment.

Key Voices

Tarana Burke

Tarana Burke's "Me Too" message raised awareness about the prevalence of sexual violence toward women and girls. Burke is still working to support survivors of sexual violence. She directs a nonprofit organization that helps girls fight injustice in their communities and succeed in their personal lives.

Looking to the Future

Today, women around the world have positions of power. There are women in most areas of work. It may seem that women have achieved equality. The truth is much different.

Women in the 1970s paved the way for equal pay, leading to Equal Pay acts. But still, women around the world make about 77 cents for every $1 a man makes. The gap is wider for non-White women. Education for girls continues to be a problem. About 130 million girls around the world do not attend school. Plan International supports girls to go to school and helps them to learn digital skills. In Saudi Arabia, women were banned from driving until 2018. The driving ban was lifted only after decades of protests by women activists—many of whom were arrested in the process.

Many Saudi Arabian women activists drove in protest of the ban. In 2011, Manal al-Sharif spent one week in jail after posting a video of herself driving. 100 women activists also joined the Women2Drive movement. They used social media to raise awareness.

New Tactics, Same Struggle

Today's feminists consider the challenges that women face because of their race, disability, sexuality, or gender identity, as well as for being women. In 2018, the United Nations stated that 80 percent of people affected by climate change are women. Tasks such as gathering food, water, and fuel are usually done by women, and these are made more difficult by the effects of climate change. Women's rights activists are involved in the fight for climate justice. The Me Too movement and the Women's March showed how the Internet can be used for campaigns. Women will continue to fight for their rights and for equality.

Key Voices

Alexandria Ocasio-Cortez

In 2018, 29-year-old Alexandria Ocasio-Cortez became the youngest woman elected to the U.S. Congress. Ocasio-Cortez is an environmental and equal rights activist. In July 2020, after receiving sexist insults from a male Representative, she spoke out about **structural sexism**. Her powerful speech drew attention to sexist and violent language toward women, and stated that only treating people with dignity and respect makes a decent man.

GET INVOLVED

Anyone can become an activist for women's rights. Here are some suggestions of how to contribute.

1 Show Support

Organizations fighting for women's rights rely on support from volunteers. Explore different organizations to find one whose aims you support, whether it's education for girls or ending violence against women. Check their website for ideas about how to support their work. Support could include sharing messages and raising awareness. It could also include fundraising and participation in events or marches.

2 Speak Out

You could help raise people's awareness about different women's rights issues. If there's a feminist group in your community, look into joining it. If not, could you start one? Write articles about women's rights for your school newspaper or website. Talk to a school librarian about setting up a feminist reading group.

3 March!

The worldwide Women's March, which started in 2017, has since grown into an international event. Check this website for annual dates, tell your friends, and go along: **www.womensmarch.com**

4 Celebrate

International Women's Day is on March 8 each year. It's a chance to celebrate women's achievements and to continue the campaign for equality. Look for events near you or celebrate in your local or school community. **www.internationalwomensday.com**

5 Volunteer

Volunteering with a women's rights organization is a great way to make a change. Many women's rights organizations rely on volunteers to help run their campaigns, whether that's by handing out leaflets or helping in the office. Use the Internet to find out about volunteer opportunities in an organization whose aims you support.

Timeline

1622 Marie de Gournay writes *Equality of Men and Women*.

1791 Olympe de Gouges publishes *Declaration of the Rights of Women and of the Female Citizen*.

1792 Mary Wollstonecraft's book *A Vindication of the Rights of Woman* is published.

1848 The Women's Rights Convention in Seneca Falls is the start of the American suffrage campaign.

1851 Sojourner Truth delivers her speech, "Ain't I a Woman," at the Women's Rights Convention in Akron, Ohio.

1893 Women in New Zealand win the right to vote.

1896 Mary Church Terrell forms the National Association of Colored Women (NACW).

1903 Emmeline Pankhurst founds the Women's Social and Political Union (WSPU) in the United Kingdom.

1918 Most Canadian women gain the right to vote. Indigenous women and men aren't able to vote until 1960.

1920 Women in the United States win the right to vote.

1956 Following years of campaigning, Egyptian women gain the right to vote.

1963 Betty Friedan's book, *The Feminine Mystique*, is published.

1963 The Equal Pay Act is passed in the United States.

1970 The Equal Pay Act is passed in the United Kingdom.

1970 On August 26, the Women's Strike for Equality takes place in New York and other American cities.

2006 Tarana Burke founds the "Me Too" movement; in 2017, the hashtag #MeToo goes viral as women protest sexual harassment and assault.

2010 UN Women forms to empower women and work for equality.

2012 Laura Bates launches the Everyday Sexism Project.

2012 Malala Yousafzai is shot by a Taliban gunman. In 2014, she becomes the youngest person to win the Nobel Peace Prize.

2014 Boko Haram kidnap 276 girls from a school in Nigeria; the Bring Back Our Girls campaign is launched.

2018 Alexandria Ocasio-Cortez, a passionate voice for women's rights, becomes the youngest woman to be elected to U.S. Congress.

2018 Women in Saudi Arabia win the right to drive following a campaign by women activists.

2020 Alexandria Ocasio-Cortez gives a speech against structural sexism.

Sources

Chapter 1

Michals, Debra. "Sojourner Truth." National Women's History Museum. 2015. https://bit.ly/2CDxJgb

Rampton, Martha. "Four Waves of Feminism." Pacific University Oregon. October 25, 2015. www.pacificu.edu/magazine/four-waves-feminism

Chapter 2

Hewitt, Nancy A. "Abolition & Suffrage." *PBS.* 1999. www.pbs.org/kenburns/not-for-ourselves-alone/abolition-suffrage

"History of Marches and Mass Actions." National Organization for Women. https://now.org/about/history/history-of-marches-and-mass-actions

Chapter 3

Cook, Beverley. "Six things you should know about the Suffragette hunger strikes." October 5, 2018. Museum of London. https://bit.ly/2EaA4zE

Chapter 4

Dismore, David M. "When Women Went on Strike: Remembering Equality Day 1970." August 26, 2010. *Ms. Magazine.* https://bit.ly/3g8jz4b

Fetters, Ashley. "The First of the 'Yale Women'." September 22, 2019. *The Atlantic.* https://bit.ly/2YabKou

"History of the Equal Rights Amendment." Alice Paul Institute. www.equalrightsamendment.org/the-equal-rights-amendment

Chapter 5

Malala Fund. https://malala.org/malalas-story

Walters, Ashley. "Sampat Pal's Gulabi Gang fights for gender revolution in India. January 25, 2015. *CBC.* https://bit.ly/3geLK1G

Yousafzai, Malala. *I am Malala.* Little Brown and Company, 2013.

Chapter 6

"Brave, Creative, Resilient: The Global State of Young Feminist Organizing." May 2017. FRIDA. https://bit.ly/3aCmdhn

Holpuch, Amanda. "Stolen daughters: what happened after #BringBackOurGirls?" October 22, 2018. *The Guardian.* https://bit.ly/3gbTaCC

Glossary

abolitionist A person who wants to stop slavery

agitate Protest for change

amendment Change to the words or meaning of a law

anonymous Not identified

assaulted Hurt or attacked by someone

Boko Haram Terrorist, armed religious group started in Nigeria

campaign To actively work in an organized way toward a political or social goal

civil rights Rights of citizens within a country no matter their race, religion, or gender

economist Someone who studies the money and resources of a place

feminism Belief that women and men should have equal rights

First Nations In Canada, Indigenous peoples who are not Métis or Inuit

gender Relating to male or female, or to any way that someone identifies

inclusive Open to everyone

Indigenous Native to, or having always lived in, a specific place

injustices Unfair or illegal treatments

lady's companion A woman, usually well educated, who lived with a woman of higher status or wealth.

lectures Talks given to a group of people to teach about a topic

lynchings Mob killings

militant Using forceful actions to achieve something

petition Document people sign to say they agree with or support something

petticoats Loose, light garments worn under a skirt or dress

racism Belief that some races or cultures are better than others

rallies Public meetings to protest or support an issue

ratified Signed or gave formal consent to; made official

reproductive rights Legal rights and freedoms concerning a person's choice about whether to reproduce, or have children

reserve In Canada, or reservation in the United States; area of land set aside for Indigenous nations or tribes

settlers People who move to a new country or area to set up a permanent home there

sexual harassment Any unwanted sexual attention, words, or acts

slavery System of people forced to work for others without pay

status In Canada, being officially recognized by government as a First Nations, Inuit, or Métis person

strike A refusal to work until demands are met

structural sexism Sexism that is embedded in social structures and laws

suffrage Right to vote

suffragettes Activists who fought for women's right to vote using militant tactics and direct action

suffragists Activists who fought for the women's right to vote usually through peaceful means

tactics Methods for achieving a goal

Taliban Religious and political group that began in Afghanistan and Pakistan and uses violence to enforce extreme views

transgender Relating to people who do not feel their gender identity matches their sex assigned to them at birth

Further Information

Books

Adichie, Chimamanda Ngozi. *We Should All Be Feminists*. New York: Anchor Books, 2015.

Hudak, Heather C. *#MeToo Movement* (Get Informed, Stay Informed). Crabtree Publishing Company, 2019.

Jensen, Kelly (editor). *Here We Are: Feminism for the Real World*. Chapel Hill, NC: Algonquin, 2017.

Lusted, Marcia Amidon. *The Fight for Women's Rights* (Activism in Action). New York: Rosen, 2019.

Messner, Kate. *Women's Right to Vote* (History Smashers). New York: Random House, 2020.

Sjonger, Rebecca. *Susan B. Anthony: On a woman's right to vote* (Deconstructing Powerful Speeches). Crabtree Publishing Company, 2019.

Websites

malala.org
The website of the Malala Fund, explaining how it supports education for girls around the world.

https://metoomvmt.org/learn-more
Learn more about the Me Too Movement and the problem of sexual violence faced by women around the world.

https://now.org/blog/10-black-feminists-you-need-to-know-about
An introduction to 10 important Black women activists.

www.unwomen.org/en/digital-library/multimedia/2016/3/timeline-womens-footprint-in-history
An interactive timeline that highlights a selection of women's rights activists through history.

www.voicesofyouth.org/meet-girls-standing-womens-rights-around-world
Profiles of some young women's rights activists who are campaigning for change today.

womenshistory.si.edu/herstory/activism
Visit this website for a history of women's activism in the United States

Index